Prayer 101

Intimacy with God

Darryl L. Gay

ISBN 979-8-88616-261-5 (paperback)
ISBN 979-8-88616-262-2 (digital)

Christian Faith Publishing
832 Park Avenue
Meadville, PA 16335
www.christianfaithpublishing.com

Printed in the United States of America

To my wife, First Lady Mireille Pierre-Louis Gay, I praise the Lord for using you to teach and inspire me not to just finish this project but finish every work that the Lord requires of me in the future. Your drive and tenacity inspire me to push harder than ever for greatness. He used you, your patience, and your unconditional love to bring me out of deep darkness and depression; and I am forever grateful to the Lord for bringing you into my life when I needed you most. You have all my heart, love, and gratitude forever.

To my former wife of twenty-nine years, Prophetess and Pastor Elaine Martin Gay, whom the Lord used to encourage and teach me by example how to share His unconditional love with others. She passed and went to be with the Lord on August 8, 2021, which left me heartbroken. I know you are cheerleading for me to complete this work that you were a vital part of from its inception. To my surprise, the Lord decided to bless me with my current wife to help me restore my life and get this book across the finish line.

Contents

Prayer for the believer is pivotal. Those who believe understand that prayer is communication with God, but most will admit that their prayer life needs improvement. Many are secretly distressed over their prayer relationship with God. They have prayed consistently and experience limited or no results at all. Therefore, they have decided that the time to pray is when they are in trouble or when life throws them a curveball. For many, frustration and even resentment have developed within the heart of their spirits toward God. They love God, but often feel that He does not care about their everyday circumstances. Often, they feel that the little things happening in their lives are too trivial for a God who is so busy dealing with huge issues. However, they hope that He cares about the major moments in their lives. As a result, many are literally holding on to their relationship with God by a thread. If one more prayer request goes unanswered, they may completely turn away from God. Unfortunately, churches all over America and the world are full of people with this experience and mindset. They have not considered that unanswered prayer is not an indictment against God but against their lack of understanding concerning prayer. Many do not understand or realize that God will not violate *His Word* just to answer their prayer. *His Word* is more valuable to Him than His name.[1] Therefore, we have a dilemma when it comes to prayer. We do not want to come out and say that it is God's fault that all our prayers are not being answered, and we do not want to blame ourselves either.

The challenge that many in the faith have is that they know others who seem to always get every prayer answered. Although they try to show joy and support for them when they are bragging on what God has done in their lives, they still find themselves irritated because their personal testimony is that God never seems to answer their prayers. Instead of them getting closer to God, often this frustration propels them further from God. Their failure to understand the plethora of SCRIPTURES revealing God's desire to have an intimate relationship with them only exacerbates the situation.[2] Therefore, they tend to view Christianity as a bunch of rules to keep, and then they tell themselves why try to keep all these rules when it is obvious that God does not care about them. Their lackadaisical walk continues to spiral downward until there is no longer a walk. They mistakenly leave the narrow path that leads to eternal life and transition to the wide and broad path that leads to eternal death and separation from the very God they claim to love.[3] From their perspective, they want a God who loves them as much as they love Him. They have literally convinced themselves that if God really loved them, why did He not answer their prayers and allow such and such to happen? Where was God when that bad thing happened that I prayed and prayed against? They feel dejected and often rejected by the God they love the most. They do not understand that everything in God's kingdom work by LAWS. They are submitted to the natural LAWS that govern our physical universe daily but have not considered that there are spiritual LAWS that govern the kingdom of God.

As Christian leaders, it is our responsibility to identify and help those who are in this downward spiral toward destruction without appearing or sounding judgmental. We are to restore them to right relationship with God from a heart of love.[4] We must willingly seek them out and train them how to effectively pray so that they can get the results that they only hear about. We must teach and convince them of the LAWS governing the kingdom of God and explain to them that the King of kings will not violate the LAWS of His kingdom for anyone. Once we realize that many are at the end of their rope, our love for Christ will compel us to help them. Christ's original disciples understood a truth that seem to have been forgotten or overlooked by the subsequent generations of believers, and that is the need for teaching when it comes to prayer. They never asked Jesus to teach them how to preach, teach, heal the sick, or even perform miracles; but they did ask Him to teach them to pray.[5] They realized that the secret to a successful personal relationship or ministry started with intimate prayer with the Father. Therefore, we as leaders must work diligently to first learn how to pray successfully and then how to disseminate this gathered information to those who need it the most.

CHAPTER I

Purpose of Prayer

IF YOU ASK MOST BELIEVERS THE PURPOSE of prayer, they will immediately inform you that it is to spend time communicating with God to inform Him of their wants and needs so that He will grant them. From their perspective, prayer is about receiving from God based on their own selfish desires. If you challenged them to think that prayer is more about giving to God than receiving, they will look at you with disbelief. They have been conditioned by previous generations and misuse of SCRIPTURE that God wants to give them everything that their heart desires.[6] Since this is the case, they develop a wish list that they recite to God every time they pray. They remind Him of HIS WORD and their expectancy to receive from Him all that they have prayed for. They have been taught that if they ask and keep on asking, that eventually God will become tired of their insistent begging and will comply to their request.[7] They never consider that God might want to answer that prayer for every human on the planet who is dealing with the same thing they are. Instead of praying for all who have that issue, which would be a selfless prayer, they are content to pray selfishly about their issue and then have the audacity to get an attitude with God if He does not answer that prayer quickly enough or to their satisfaction.

Secondly, many will inform you that for them, the purpose of prayer is to pray for forgiveness for the sins they have committed. They realize their imperfections; therefore, they want to do everything within their power to keep their slate clean with God so that He does not punish them for their wrongdoing. Most with this mindset are not willing to do what is necessary to avoid willful sinning. Their mission is to make sure they ask for forgiveness after committing the sin.[8] They make statements like, *"God understands I am doing the best I can"* or *"God knows my heart,"* to explain their continued sinful behavior. For them prayer is very important because it is the mechanism used to cleanse their conscience. Those who ascribe to this way of thinking believe that unanswered prayer is the result of unconfessed sin. So they rack their brains, trying to remember all the sins they have committed so that they can pray and get them covered under the blood of Jesus. That way, they are convinced that God will answer their prayer once all their sins are covered and forgiven. If something bad occurs to them or someone else, immediately they will think and possibly say that it is because of some sinful act of disobedience they have done. From their perspective, the blessings and favor of God are contingent upon what they say and do and not what Jesus did on the cross for them.

Prayer does have a purpose, and it is beyond the two things that most believe. Prayer is a major part of a personal relationship developed with God, the One whom we love with all our heart. Therefore, prayer to the believer is supposed to be a conversation steeped in love. This love is to flow both ways, and this love is meant to be unconditional. Often, we hear about the unconditional (agape) love that the Father has for us and we realize from *SCRIPTURE* that this love was proven by His sending His only begotten Son to pay our sin debt by dying on the cross for us.[9] Yet for most, it is never considered that our love toward Him and the humans He has created should also be unconditional. This means that there is nothing God can do or allow to happen to you that should affect your love for Him. Even when the enemy uses people to attack and mistreat you, you understand that because of your unconditional love for the Father, that you will comply with *HIS WORD* and forgive them.[10] You will even pray for and bless them because of your unconditional love for the Father[11] As you live your life, you are daily reminded as you look at your imperfections that the Father loves you unconditionally. Therefore, you love Him with all your heart, spirit, soul, mind, body, and strength because you realize that while you were a sinner, Christ died to pay the penalty for your sins.[12] You appreciate what He did so much that all you can do is love Him unconditionally. It takes this level of unconditional love to be able to make the statement, *"Not My will but Your will be done."*[13] True prayer only occurs when the believer can make this statement and faithfully live with the results.

Another purpose of prayer is to teach the believer discipline. We cannot truly be His disciples if we do not learn discipline. Unfortunately, many in the world seem to understand and practice more discipline than believers. They will modify their eating habits for the sake of being healthy. They will work diligently to condition their bodies through exercising on a consistent basis. Many will discipline themselves by obtaining difficult degrees from higher institutes of learning such as colleges or universities. They seem to understand that an achieved result requires time, and they are willing to invest that time for their dream to become a reality. As believers, we can learn a lot from this mindset conveyed by many who do not ascribe themselves to the tenets of Christianity. It takes patience to pray and then wait for a response. It takes even more patience to receive the desired response to the prayer and then having to wait for it to manifest. The days, weeks, months, seasons, and even years teaches discipline. We learned prior to salvation how to behave selfishly. This behavior shows up as impatience and produces undisciplined behavior. Often a bad attitude is revealed because we become tired of waiting on God to answer. Sometimes we become real spiritual and say we need more patience and even go so far as to pray for it, not realizing that we are grieving the heart of God because we have chosen not to trust Him to come through for us at the right time. Those who operate this way clearly do not understand that they are not supposed to just sit around and wait, but rather they are to be serving the Lord with gladness while waiting.[14] As Jesus stated many eons ago, the harvest is plentiful but the labors are few.[15] There is much work to be done in the kingdom while we patiently wait for our Commander in Chief to answer our prayers.

Often, people say character is who you are when no one is watching. Well, another purpose of prayer is to teach character to the believer. Because so much time is being spent in prayer with the Father, it is literally impossible to not become more like Him. Even reading and studying *His Word* is meant to transition the way we as believers think.[16] Therefore, when we spend time in His presence praying, we are guaranteed that it is His plan to change us. Unfortunately, many believers do not realize that a major purpose of prayer is to spend time in the presence of an Almighty God. Instead, they often see prayer as the means to obtain an expected end. Again, they are only praying because they want something from God that they are not able to obtain without Him. Usually, prayer only occurs after they have exhausted every other possible way of achieving their desire. The concept of spending time in His presence is foreign and often frightening to them. We must remember that many have been conditioned to believe that God is out to get them and punish them for all the wrong they have done and are currently doing. Therefore, they are afraid that if they had a one-on-one dialogue with God, it would not go too well. For them, it is better to just pray to Him and tell Him what they want/need and then move on to the next thing on their list for that day. They do not understand that the purpose of spending time in His presence is for Him to literally transform us into the image of His Son.[17] The Father wants to see Himself in us. Jesus stated that He only did what He saw the Father doing and only said what He heard the Father saying.[18] This is literally the place where God desires for all His children to be. As His sons and daughters, we are to exhibit His character in all our dealings, but this will only occur based on the amount of time we are willing to spend in His presence. Once we understand that His unconditional love for us is truly unconditional, we will find ourselves running to get into His presence instead of running from His presence.

A development of prayer is that we who sincerely practice it will hear His voice. Understanding this truth will help you to realize that God does not want you to be confused concerning His plan for each moment of your life. His desire is for prayer to be a two-way conversation between two who love one another madly and unconditionally.

He stated in *SCRIPTURE* that His sheep would know or recognize His voice and a stranger's voice they would not follow.[19] It is imperative to God that we as His disciples can discern or distinguish His voice from the voice of the enemy and from the voice of our fleshly nature. We must remember that our failure to determine His voice reveals a lack of relationship with the Father. We must willingly and faithfully spend more time in His presence so that we can learn His voice. For example, most will admit that they know their mother's or child's voice even in a crowded room. This can be said because they have spent enough quality time with them to know their voice. Likewise, the more time we spend with God in prayer and in *HIS WORD* the more we are guaranteed to know His voice when He speaks. Once He speaks, we are compelled by *SCRIPTURE* to comply by becoming submissive and obedient to what He tells us to do.[20] The wrong definition of prayer makes it about your telling Him what to do. Those who do that soon realize that what they are asking for usually never occurs. When we go to God seeking what He wants for us, we are guaranteed that He will meet and supply our every need.[21] We can trust Him completely. He said if we are willing and obedient, we will eat the good of the land.[22] A unique blessing is available for those who are willing to operate from a place of obedience.

CHAPTER 2

Hindrances to Prayer

As believers, we all must admit that there are times when we feel our prayers are being hindered from coming to pass. Admitting this publicly is very difficult. We usually admit to ourselves privately, and then we often become frustrated with God because we do not understand why our prayers are not being answered. We have been taught that God may not come when you want Him to but that He is always on time. Yet we have waited so long that our waiting is tired of waiting. What do you do when it looks like God is never going to answer your prayers? I mean, you live as holy as you know how. You do your best to be a light and example of Christ to a lost world. Yet you do not see your prayers being answered. Often, we blame God for not answering, and we never consider that we could be praying wrong. The challenge is that most who have matured in Christ are praying for things based on the SCRIPTURES and still we see hindrances. This confusion breeds frustration and sometimes hostility toward God. However, this hostility often shows up in how we treat others. Often, we blame our quick temper as being inherited from our genealogy when it may be that this temper is coming from our internal frustration with God Himself. Salvation is God's way of regenerating us so that the stuff from our genealogy no longer has a legal right to show up and dominate our lives. Salvation is a contract being you and God, where He replaces your DNA with His. Often, we reference this by saying we are new creations in Christ Jesus.[23]

Unfortunately, this resequencing does not mean that our prayers will be answered as timely as we would like or that they will be answered at all. Because of our great love for God, it is extremely difficult to blame Him. Therefore, we tend to just live angrily and when someone rubs us the wrong way, we figuratively bite their heads off. They leave from our presence confused and wonder if that is what being a Christian is, then they do not want any part of it. They do not realize, and usually we do not either, that we are struggling with internal frustration that we are not able to fully understand or verbalize.

PROVERBS 15:4 reveals that our words are meant to build up and encourage others. When frustrated, it is literally impossible to encourage others. However, we must first learn to encourage and build up ourselves.[24] Until we are successful in this endeavor, we can be assured that we will not treat others right. Our relationships tend to suffer from our inability to recognize what is going on internally in our lives. Therefore, as much as we know the Golden Rule, we often fall short when trying to apply it.[25] This same *SCRIPTURE* reveals that our words are a tree of life. This is challenging because this implies that there is fruit on that tree. Once we realize that our words are fruit that is being eaten by ourselves and others, we will become much more mindful of what we say and how we say it.[26] The *BIBLE* reveals that the tree of life is eternal.[27] Our words are fruit, and we and all that we encounter are eating from the tree that is us.[28] Physical wounds heal over time, but often spoken words continue to torture our lives forever. Most people are still dealing with something negative that was said or done to them in their childhood. We must realize this and deal with all the negative words that the enemy have sent our way to demoralize and crush our spirits. We must understand that the role of the enemy is to attack us on a spiritual level because he realizes that if our spirits are crushed that our dreams and ability to fulfill our purpose and destiny will be aborted. Therefore, throughout our lives, he has sent people our way to say things that will cause us to feel bad about ourselves. He uses those words to help us not like ourselves by tricking us into believing that we would be better off if we were taller or shorter, born into a different family, hair straight or curly, skin lighter or darker, had both parents in the home to raise us or did not have both parents in the home to raise us, and the list goes on and on. His mission is to crush our spirits, and he understands that since we are created in the image and likeness of God that our words are powerful and eternal.[29] For example, God told Adam that the day in which he ate from the tree of the knowledge of good and evil that he would die.[30] The only way God could fix this was to literally kill *His Word*. *John 1:14* reveals that the *Word of God* was made flesh and dwelt (lived) among us. Thus, when Jesus died on the cross, God was killing the *Word* that He had spoken to Adam for mankind to be freed from the curse of eternal death. Unfortunately, we do not have that same power to crucify and kill the negative words that we have spoken over our lives or the words others spoke that we have made ours. We must pray to the Father in the name of Jesus and ask Him to intervene into our situation and turn this thing around. Once doing this it is incumbent upon us that we refrain from speaking words contrary to God's will and plan for our lives. Jesus stated that the words that He speak are spirit and life.[31] He also stated that He only spoke what He heard the Father speaking and only did what He saw the Father doing.[32] We, too, should work diligently to ensure that Jesus's testimony is ours too.

Additionally, as fruit grows it is affected by the elements of nature. Also, usually some type of pesticide is put on the tree itself to hinder certain insects from damaging or destroying the fruit before it is ready for harvesting. We should consider this analogy concerning the words that proceed out of our mouths. We must allow the water of the *Word of God* to wash our words so that they are pure.[33] This is the only way we can be assured that our words are not poisonous and that they will not crush the spirits of those who hear and receive them. This reveals another reason why Satan attacks all believers when it comes to reading and studying the *Bible*. He knows that if he can keep you from partaking of the *Holy Scriptures*, that your words will remain poisonous to all who hear them, including yourself. He knows that we will literally self-destruct and destroy our own destiny when we do not allow the *Word of God* to wash and cleanse our words. He then convinces us to blame others for our failures. The list to blame is numerous, and depending on your race or social economic status, he will give you the person or group of persons to blame for why you are the way you are. Usually, the list is pretty long. We tend to blame our parents for certain things and then society for others. At the same time, we quote the *SCRIPTURE*: "*I can do all things through Christ which strengtheneth me.*"[34] This reveals how confused we are in our souls. The *BIBLE* calls this dysfunction double-minded and reveals to us that we who are trapped in this dysfunction will not be able to get our prayers answered.[35] Now we know why many, if not most, of our prayers are not being answered. One day we are operating in faith; and often, before that day is over, we are operating in doubt and fear. We have allowed our emotions to trick us into believing and saying things contrary to what we have prayed. When we do this, we literally put God's angels in handcuffs. They are no longer able to bring the answers to our prayers because of our poisonous words. His angels have been commissioned by Him to obey His commandments and to hearken to the voice of *HIS WORD*.[36] Understanding this concept should cause all believers to become more mindful of the words that they allow to proceed from their mouths. The worse time to speak is when we are emotional. We have been commanded to walk by faith and not our feelings.[37] We must learn to trust God's plan to the point that we will only believe and say what *HIS WORD* says concerning whatever situation we are facing.

If we desire the full blessing and favor of God to continually manifest in our lives, we must make sure that our mouths are refraining from speaking evil words. To accomplish this supernatural feat, we must remain submitted to the Holy Spirit by allowing Him to daily tame our tongues as we allow Him to speak through us.[38] We must remain committed to daily reading and studying the *WORD OF GOD* so that it can transform our way of thinking for out of the abundance of the heart the mouth speaks.[39] If our thinking is not transformed, then our words will not be either. Lastly, we must cast down every thought that is contrary to the knowledge of who Jesus Christ is in the *HOLY SCRIPTURES* and in our own personal lives. Then we will see sustained victory pertaining to the words that proceed from our mouths. This clearly is the will of the God we love and serve. Doing this ensures that many more of our prayers will be answered because we will no longer find ourselves operating as one who is double-minded. This ensures that we will enjoy life and see good days.[40]

CHAPTER 3

Blueprint for Prayer

Studying the *Bible* extensively will reveal that there is a blueprint to everything God does. For example, when God wanted Moses to build the tabernacle, He gave him a blueprint.[41] Additionally, He even gave him a blueprint concerning the furniture that would be used in the tabernacle, and He was very specific concerning what the priests would wear.[42] God is a God of details. When we view nature, we can see how detailed God is. For example, He uses a basic design for animals, and then He makes variations to produce a multiplicity of different species. All the warm-blooded animals would have similar characteristics as would all the cold-blooded animals. However, there are similarities between the two types because God used a common pattern or blueprint for all animals. Often this common blueprint breeds confusion in the hearts of nonbelievers that causes them to believe that all animals derived from a lower species of animal. The process is known as the theory of evolution. The dilemma is that evolution takes millions of years to occur, and therefore, faith is required to believe because there is no evidence of transitional species. For example, they believe that there is a common ancestor between humans and monkeys/apes, but the fossil record disagrees with their theory. However, we as humans have been created to look for the blueprint in all things. Unfortunately, most nonbelievers are not aware that our Creator placed this desire inside of us to understand how He has done what He has done. It would behoove all to become more aware of the God who has developed a blueprint for all things seen and unseen.[43]

Once we realize that God has a blueprint for everything He has ever done, we will come to appreciate the fact that there is also a blueprint for prayer. Those who are successful in prayer have learned and follow the blueprint provided them by the Lord in *His Word*. All people want their prayers to be answered, but most have been tricked into believing that you can go to God in prayer and just speak how you feel and expect Him to come through for you. As we read this book, we are learning that this is not always the case. The blueprint to prayer is not hidden from humanity. God put it in the *Holy Bible*. Jesus's disciples asked Him to teach them to pray as John had taught his disciples to pray.[44] They understood that successful prayer could only occur if they allowed themselves to be taught. They realized that the secret to Jesus's power was His prayer life. We must remember that when Jesus prayed, He usually prayed alone. Whether He rose early in the morning before daybreak or late in the evening, He would always go to a solidarity place to pray.[45] He spent quality time in the presence of the Father. The hours spent with the Father in prayer was evidenced in how He would only do the will of the Father. As His disciples watched Him, they realized that His secret to success was based on what He was doing in His private time. Since they were not privy to what He was saying while alone with the Father, they humbled themselves and asked to be taught. The twelve disciples had a private conversation based on a need they realized they had. They were people who had spent most of their lives praying without success as well. They noticed that whenever Jesus prayed, the Father answered affirmably. After seeing this occur repeatedly, they concluded that Jesus knew something about prayer that they did not. Now came the decision to decide if they wanted to ask Him. They had to humble themselves to ask the question that most are not willing to ask. For them it was simple, either continue to pray without positive results for the rest of their lives or humble themselves and ask for help.

The decision to ask for the blueprint of prayer changed their lives. Jesus immediately revealed the blueprint of prayer to them.

He started out by saying when you pray, pray like this.[46] He did not tell them to memorize the blueprint as most Christians have done. He did not tell them to repeat/pray the blueprint either as most are taught to do. Instead, He said pray based on this pattern or blueprint. He gave the elements required to pray successfully. When thinking of a blueprint, I can remember seeing as a child the blueprints for a building. Everything on the blueprint was scaled to fit on the piece of paper. What was on the paper represented a very large structure that would later be built once the architect had completed the design. No one lives or work in the blueprint. For the most part the only person who truly appreciates that blueprint is the architect and those who will follow the blueprint to build the house or building. The enemy of our souls have tricked us into trying to live in the blueprint instead of understanding that the purpose of the blueprint is to reveal to us a much larger edifice that is to be built through prayer. In the spirit realm, God wants to establish His kingdom here on earth, but to do so, He needs us to pray based on the blueprint and not just pray the blueprint. We cannot build His kingdom on the blueprint, but we can and should build His kingdom based upon the things revealed in the blueprint.

Thus, He said pray, *"Our Father which are in heaven."* The first thing to notice is Jesus wanted His disciples to know who they were praying to and where He was located. By informing them that the Father was in heaven implied that He is not controlled by the four-dimensional world wherein we live. According to science, the four-dimensional world is made up of length, width, height/depth, and time. Therefore, whatever occurs in our universe has no power or authority over Him. When we pray, we have confidence that He can circumvent whatever is going on in our universe. Secondly, Jesus stated that the name of the Father is to be hallowed (made holy). Understanding that we are reaching out in prayer to a God who is holy informs us that He has no evil in Him nor does He desire to bring evil into our lives.[47] Therefore, the negative that has occurred in our lives has been derived from the devil. Then we are to pray for the kingdom of God to be manifested on earth as it is already manifested in heaven. Praying this part of the blueprint shifts us from under the authority of the rules of this physical universe and under the authority of our Creator. We become His responsibility. Within this concept of His kingdom being established is that His divine will be revealed and incorporated on earth as it is already revealed and incorporated in heaven. Now the blueprint reveals ownership from this point forward. We now pray for God to provide daily sustenance for us. This is not just physical food, but also spiritual and mental. God's desire is for us to prosper in all areas of our lives.[48] Now we ask for forgiveness of our sins or misdeeds based on our ability to forgive those who have wronged us. We understand from SCRIPTURE that if we refuse to forgive others God will not forgive us.[49] We ask our King not to lead us into temptation. This request reveals ownership. You can only lead what you have control of. Additionally, we are commanded to request that we are not delivered into the hands of the evil one. Again, this also shows ownership. The end of the blueprint instructs us to remind God that we are part of His kingdom and in that kingdom, He has all the power, glory, and authority and that His reign over His kingdom is eternal.

CHAPTER 4

Types of Prayer

GOD IS SO AMAZING THAT HE HAS provided multiple types of prayer to address whatever issue we may have. From God's perspective, He expects His children to pray without ceasing.[50] Another SCRIPTURE given by Jesus said we should always pray and not lose hope.[51] Prayer requires perseverance as we patiently wait for God to answer. As believers and kingdom citizens it is our responsibility to keep the communication lines between ourselves and our King always open. Once we realize and understand that it is a privilege to talk to Him, we will share our heart with Him completely. We will no longer use prayer as a *wish list*, but rather, we will spend our time in prayer seeking the voice of God so that we can pray what is on His mind. We will throw our *wish list* away and pray from God's *wish list* because we know that He knows what we need before we ask and that He will always meet and supply every need.[52] He promised in *HIS WORD* that He is the God of more than enough (Jehovah-Jireh). Therefore, we should continually trust Him to go above and beyond when it comes to meeting and fulfilling our needs.[53] Furthermore, we should focus on praying God's will, realizing that He has given us multiple types of prayer to pray so that we may please Him.

In this chapter, we will highlight and discuss many types of prayer, but the most important prayer to pray from God's perspective is the prayer of repentance. This is the first message that both John the Baptist and Jesus preached.[54] We are to come before God with a repentant heart and pray for forgiveness of the sins we have committed. Before we get too holy in our minds and say we have not sinned, the *BIBLE* teaches that all have sinned and fall short of God's glory.[55] Also, *SCRIPTURE* teaches that the one who states he has no sin is living in deception.[56] Furthermore, when the woman caught in the very act of adultery was brought to Him to be judged and condemned, Jesus gave permission for them to condemn her based on the idea that they could if they had no sin in their lives. According to the *WORD OF GOD*, all left without stoning her because they realized they all had active sin in their lives.[57] As wicked as the Pharisees and Sadducees were, on this one occasion, they allowed the Holy Spirit to bring conviction upon them, and they realized that they too were guilty of sin and had areas in their lives that required repentance. *To repent means to have a change of mind concerning what was done and to decide never to do it again.* Unfortunately, most never truly repent because, when asking for forgiveness, they already know that they plan to commit the sin again. Imagine how this mindset breaks the heart of our loving Father. Repentance is only attainable when we truly purpose in our hearts never to do it again, no matter how much we may want to. God smiles when we permanently turn away from the temptation because He has made a way of escape for us.[58]

Secondly, we are commanded in *SCRIPTURE* to confess our faults one to another so that we may be healed.[59] God's goal is to help His kingdom kids to step out of denial and to become honest about what they are facing. Moreover, *1 JOHN 1:9* commands us to repent before God. Now we are challenged to bring our sin or weakness before our brothers and sisters. There is something released in the spirit realm when we are open with one another. We make ourselves accountable to others and give them permission to speak into our lives. The *BIBLE* teaches that iron sharpens iron.[60] The only way we can sharpen one another is to allow our lives to touch. We do this by opening up to one another, and by doing so, the rough places and abrasions that have become a part of our lives can be rubbed away. True love will reveal itself when we make a conscious decision to operate in openness and sincerity. As believers, we must make ourselves into a safe place where people can confess without fear of judgment or persecution. Where we are strong, we are to strengthen those who are weak, while realizing that God will bring others along to strengthen us in our areas of weakness. The *BIBLE* clearly teaches that we all will reap what we have sown.[61] Therefore, it behooves us all to become a safe place where others can confess their faults and receive the spiritual, mental, and emotional healing that Jesus died on the cross for them to receive.

To really appreciate and appropriate the prayer of binding and loosing into our lives as believers, we must understand our place in the kingdom of God. As kingdom citizens, we should only pray from a place or position of influence. We are seated in heavenly places with Christ Jesus.[62] From a spiritual perspective, we are seated next to the throne of God. Therefore, it is our responsibility to observe what we are seeing in heaven and pray for the manifestation of that on earth.[63] However, before praying for what we see there to manifest here, we must realize that there are things occurring here that are not occurring there, and it is our responsibility as kingdom citizens to bind them up by taking authority over them. As kingdom citizens, we have been given the responsibility of managing the earth in the same way our King is managing heaven.[64] We have been given dominion over the earth, and as kings, we are to make declarations that are in line with *GOD'S WORD* and will and then expect them to occur. Christ has given us the keys to the kingdom.[65] Therefore, what we lock on earth is locked in heaven and what we unlock on earth is unlocked in heaven.

A major part of the life of a believer is praying for those who have been attacked by sickness and disease. Often the malady faced is a result of bad behavior and not properly taking care of one's self. However, as believers it is not our place to judge but to pray. The prayer of faith or the prayer of the faithful will bring healing and deliverance to those who are facing sickness and disease.[66] When we pray this type of prayer, we are assured by God Himself that He will heal them and forgive them of the sins they have committed against Him. Jesus stated that we will always have the poor with us.[67] What this means is that there will always be people who need prayer. Poor does not just mean lack of physical resources, but it refers to the curse placed upon humanity because of the sin of Adam. Christ freed us from the curse of sin and death when He died on the cross, arose from the dead, and ascended back to the right side of the Father in heaven.[68] Unfortunately, many in the family do not realize that they are free and that healing is just a prayer away. We understand that when we believe and pray this way that we are giving all the glory for the breakthrough to God and we have confidence He will act.

The prayer of supplication is the one type of prayer believers are most familiar with. It is the prayer of asking God for things that we deem needful. Amazingly *SCRIPTURE* commands us to make our requests known unto our Lord.[69] He has promised to meet and supply all our needs according to His riches in glory.[70] He has promised that He will open the windows of heaven and allow downpours of blessing to manifest into the lives of those who faithfully obey *HIS WORD*.[71] Although we know that obedience opens the windows of heaven, often we as humans try partial obedience because of our fleshly love of sin and hope that will be enough to get God to still bless us. Out of His heart of love, He will allow some blessings to fall into our lives even when we have not given ourselves completely to Him. The Syro-Phenician woman was able to get her daughter healed off a crumb that fell from the Master's table.[72] However, we have been told that it is God's will for His children to sit at the King's table and eat lavishly.[73] Unfortunately, many are pleased to just get a crumb when the contents on the entire table is available for them.

The prayer of thanksgiving is probably the least prayed type of prayer because the enemy of our souls has tricked most to believe that they deserve everything they have due to their own righteousness. We have ways of justifying our actions whether those actions are good or evil.[74] We tend to remind God of what we have done for Him and why we deserve all the blessings He has given and more. Often, we get attitude with God for not giving us everything we ask for. However, we are commanded in *SCRIPTURE* to give thanks to Him. So much so we are informed that it is the will of God concerning humanity that we thank Him.[75] Often believers say I do not know God's will for my life. Well, it starts with thanking Him for all that He has done for us. Once we realize that every breath is a gift from

God, we will become more thankful. We have been conditioned to take so much for granted. We all should repent for this mindset and practice thanking Him more often for all the wonderful things He has already done for us and the ones we love.

In recent years, there has been more of an emphasis put upon worship in the body of Christ. The prayer of worship does not thank God for what He has done but for who He is. When we pray this way, we focus on the *Isness* of who God is. We bow before the Great I Am and remind Him of who He is. We treat Him as the Sovereign King as we faithfully bow before Him. We understand that because of His holiness, we must bow in His presence. When this type of prayer is prayed, we do not ask for anything from Him. We consider it such and honor and privilege to spend time in His presence that we just desire to bask in His glory. Often worship music is used to help us get into this mindset. We may even prostrate ourselves before Him to show Him how humble we are as we come before Him. This type of prayer requires complete focus on Him and not what we are facing. Repentance is also necessary if we are going to enter the presence of a Holy God.

The least type of prayer prayed by believers is the prayer of consecration. This is when we pray, *"Not My will but Your will be done."*[76] Honestly, this is the most difficult prayer to pray because it requires surrendering our plans, desires, and will to the Lord. It means that we trust His Wisdom over ours. It means that we have come to the place where we are willing to accept His plan for us no matter the outcome. Although He told us in *His Word* that His plans for us are good, it is still difficult to completely trust Him.[77] Trusting His plan is extremely difficult on a plethora of levels. It is like jumping out of a plane without a parachute. You can see the ground coming quickly at you, and you know that without a parachute, the end is near. God's goal is for us to reach our end, so that He may prove to us that our end is His beginning for us. This new beginning causes greater consecration to God as we trust His Spirit to lead, guide, and direct us into all truth. Since it is impossible for God to fail us, we should accept and expect His will to be accomplished in our yielded lives. We should always remember that a yielded life ensures a life full of answered prayers.

The easiest prayer for believers to pray is the prayer of imprecation, which means praying against one's enemies. We all have a doctorate degree in this type of prayer. King David exercised this type of prayer often in the book of *Psalms*. We too have prayed this way too many times ourselves. However, this is wrong praying, and God cannot and will not answer prayers that are prayed outside His will. We have been commanded to pray blessings upon our enemies.[78] However, it is more natural to pray judgment upon them. We want the Sovereign God to give them what they deserve or better yet for Him to turn His back for a little while so that we can give them what they deserve. When we are thinking this way, we have forgotten that our fight is not a flesh and blood fight.[79] The war we face is spiritual, and the foe is Satan and his kingdom of fallen angels and demons. All the prayers King David prayed in the *Psalms* can and should be used against the kingdom of darkness and not people.[80] Once we make a difference in our hearts between the person and the spirit that used them to commit the evil against us, we can properly apply *Scripture* by blessing them and cursing the evil spirit that used them to bring the harm or hurt upon us. This principle is much easier to understand than implement because the enemy will always try to keep you seeing the person as evil instead of the evil spirit using them. Maturity is required to master praying and blessing a person when every part of your mind is telling you to do the opposite. The blessing awaits those who make praying for their enemies their priority.

The prayer of commitment is another type of prayer that most believers are aware of. Those who were raised in church were taught to bring their burdens and problems to the altar and leave them there. When the pastor would have altar call, all were encouraged to come to the altar to pray. Leaving the burden at the altar was easy in the moment of emotion. However, when faced with the temptation of carrying that problem later, often most were overwhelmed. It seemed that God would not answer the prayer or remove the burden fast enough, and then we would take it upon ourselves to try to fix it ourselves. As stated, most are aware of this type of prayer, but unfortunately, most have not mastered it. It is our human nature to try to fix things even those we know are beyond our power to fix. Knowing this concept has not helped us to patiently wait upon the Lord to handle it for us. We cast our cares on Him initially because we are convinced that He cares for us.[81] Over time it becomes more difficult to do this because we often allow Satan to convince us that since God has not come through yet that He will not. We must constantly remind ourselves that those who wait upon the Lord will mount upon wings like eagles, that they will run and not grow weary, that they shall walk and not faint.[82]

The most powerful type of prayer is often overlooked or completely misunderstood. The prayer of agreement or corporate prayer is the type of prayer that the enemy despises the most. He under stands and knows the power of agreement for he has caused humans to use it against God before. The tower of Babel is an example of this. The people came together corporately as one, and if the Triune Godhead had not intervened, they would have been able to get to heaven without God.[83] Satan's mission is to keep the church universal, and the church locally at odds with one another over issues that does not even matter when it comes to moving heaven with our prayers. The *BIBLE* calls us the body of Christ and goes so far as to say that although we have different functions, all those functions are necessary and should not be minimized.[84] *SCRIPTURE* reveals that one of us can cause one thousand demons to leave, and that two of us can cause ten thousand demons to leave a situation.[85] We have such authority when we come together in agreement. We are promised when just two of us come together in His name that there will be three there.[86] He promised to come and intervene into our situation when just two of us are gathered in agreement. When we pray corporately, we are praying as one man before our God, and we are assured by Him that what we seek He will do. The early church understood this, and it is recorded in the book of *ACTS* that as they prayed as one man, that the entire building shook. The power of agreement is the one thing Satan fears the most and is the one thing we are believers must embrace the most.

The prayer of intercession may be the least type of prayer prayed. We as humans are wired to be selfish, and this trait does not disappear when we accept Jesus Christ as our Lord, Savior and Master. Instead, it often leads to our praying selfishly: only praying for our family members and close friends. Selfish prayers do not please our Heavenly Father and His Christ. *JOHN 17* shows how Jesus interceded for the church. It is a model that we as believers should adhere to. We are commanded in the *NEW TESTAMENT* to pray for one another.[87] We must learn to take this to the next dimension if we are going to be the intercessors that God is calling for in this last and evil day. Instead of praying for one person with a sin deficiency, sickness or disease, we must learn to pray for all people on earth who are dealing with that situation. Then we are attacking the demonic force that has been released by Satan himself to attack myriads of people. As intercessors, our mission is to take authority over demonic spirits and strongholds and cast them into the pit of hell so that they cannot attack and harm humans any longer. We have been tricked by the enemy into believing that intercessory prayer is only for a few believers who are seasoned, older, and without much else to do. However, all believers have been commanded by our Commander in Chief to make intercession for others.[88] As loyal citizens of His kingdom, we must faithfully and obediently adhere to His command, and we will see immediate results as we pray the heart of God.

The most important type of prayer is praying in the Spirit. This is the greatest weapon of prayer we have been given by our Lord and Savior Jesus Christ. He promised He would not leave us comfortless but would send us another Comforter who would lead, guide and direct us into all truth.[89] He assured His disciples that this Comforter had been with them but would soon live within them.[90] He also informed them that the Holy Spirit would not speak of Himself but that He would elevate Jesus Christ in the heart of the believer.[91] Unfortunately, praying in the Spirit or speaking in unknown tongues (languages) is the least understood and used type of prayer. Although the *BIBLE* gives specific guidelines on how to pray in the Spirit, many denominations have decided that it is not to be used at all in the church service, and many have gone so far as to say it should not be used at all.[92] They have literally made prayer into a mental robotic exercise where they are completely in charge of what will be prayed. Yet we are told that there are times when we do not know what to pray for as we ought and that it is at those times that the Holy Spirit will pray through us what is the will of the Father.[93] For God's kingdom to manifest here on earth, someone here must say what He is saying there. The Holy Spirit is God on earth who desires to pray the will of the Father, but He needs your permission and your vocal cords. The model prayer given by Jesus to His disciples commanded us to pray for His kingdom to operate in power and authority on earth as it is in heaven.[94] Since we have not experienced heaven in our knowledge, we cannot fully articulate what the kingdom of God is like. We have *SCRIPTURE* to help us understand, but as the Apostle John revealed in the book of *REVELATION*, our understanding pales in comparison to what heaven is like.[95] Therefore, it behooves us to operate in obedience by allowing the Holy Spirit to pray through us as He wills. The Apostle Paul stated that praying and singing in the Spirit would occur as he willed.[96] He understood that praying in an unknown language was just like praying in a known language. He would make the decision; and whenever he decided to pray in tongues, which was often, that the Holy Spirit would take over and pray through Him. Jesus Christ is waiting for the entire body to make the same decision so that His kingdom can be manifested in fullness on earth. Praying in the Spirit gives the Holy Spirit the opportunity to pray all types of prayer through us so that the will of the Father may be fulfilled here on earth.

CHAPTER 5

Prayers in the Bible

WE HAVE ESTABLISHED THE IMPORTANCE OF PRAYER throughout this book. Now we will look at some pivotal prayers recorded in the *HOLY SCRIPTURES* so that we can verify that we are always praying according to His will. We have a promise that when we pray according to His will that He hears us and answers our petition.[97] We must remember that the God we serve desires to bless us beyond measure. At the same time, we must understand that He will not violate *HIS WORD* to bless us. Therefore, it behooves us to learn the patterns developed in the *SCRIPTURES* concerning prayer to ensure that when we pray, we pray prayers that God can answer. Again, we are assured that when we do this, He will answer because of the great love He has for His sons and daughters. We will now look at some *biblical* examples to help us understand that even when we are not faithful concerning our prayer life that God is always faithful to *HIS WORD* and will for our lives.

We chronicle the adult life of Abraham as revealed in the *WORD OF GOD*. We do not meet him as a boy, or even a young man. When we meet him, he is already married and approaching the age of seventy-five.[98] We are introduced to him as he is introduced to the God of heaven. He is instructed to leave all that he knows and to start walking and as he walks God will lead him.[99] Abraham is married; but Sarah, his wife, is barren. Abraham wants a son more than anything. This is revealed as he brings his deceased brother's son, Lot, with him on the journey.[100] This was not according to God's will, so He allows conflict to occur between those working for Abraham and Lot. This conflict caused separation with Lot moving his family towards Sodom and Gomorrah.[101] Now Abraham turned his attention to one of his servants Eliezer of Damascus to be a son unto him.[102] God interrupted his thoughts by informing him that he and his wife would have a son.[103] Unfortunately, it took God too long to fulfill His promise, so he and his wife decided to help God out by giving Sarah's maid to Abraham in marriage.[104] Now he has a son from the maid Hagar named Ismael.[105] Now his attention is turned toward this son. Then God visits again to correct his thoughts and inform him again that what He said many years earlier concerning he and Sarah having a son was still going to happen.[106] Now the covenant of circumcision is given to him, and once the extra flesh is removed, he and his wife conceive and bring forth Isaac.[107] God answered the prayer that was deep in Abraham's heart. It took twenty-five years, but the joy that flooded Abraham and Sarah's heart made the wait worthwhile.

Unlike Abraham, when it comes to Moses, we chronicle his entire life. We meet him as a baby who has God's favor on his life.[108] As a result, he is saved when all the boy babies of the Hebrews are being killed. Through amazing circumstances, he is raised in the house of Pharaoh when all know that he is a Hebrew.[109] His actions at forty reveals that at some level he knows his purpose and is willing to fulfill it. He kills an Egyptian to protect one of his fellow Hebrews.[110] This act of murder causes him to run for his life and to spend the next forty years of his life in the land of Midian, where he marries and has two sons.[111] However, he abandoned his faith during this time and was just existing. In the fulness of time, God interrupted his meager existence and offered him the opportunity to fulfill his destiny. By that time, Moses was unsure of himself and filled with many doubts concerning his destiny. God helped him pass them all and instructed him that instead of delivering the Hebrews one at a time he would deliver them all at once.[112] To his surprise, his brother Aaron, who he had not seen in forty years, had escaped and was headed to visit him.[113] Unfortunately, Moses had wasted the time given by God to work on his character and temper. Ultimately, this was the cause of his not being able to fulfill his purpose.[114] He was successful in getting the people out of Egypt, but he got them stuck in the wilderness. When they would really upset him, he would pray to God concerning them, usually blaming God for them being the way they were.[115] God would continually tell him that the people belonged to him.[116] He finally realized that God was right, and when God spoke about destroying them all because of their continued disobedience, Moses prayed for them.[117] Although Moses allowed his temper to get the best of him by striking the rock twice when God told him to only speak to the rock, he prayed to God for Him to provide a successor to take the Hebrews into the Promised Land.[118] In the end, he learned how important it is to pray prayers according to God's ultimate will. As a result, his successor, Joshua, was able to get the people into the Promised Land.

We meet Samson prior to his birth due to the barrenness of his mother.[119] Samson is extremely unique because, although he is the son of a miracle, like Isaac, there is a Nazarite vow placed upon his life that restricts him from eating and touching certain things.[120] We are not told much about his childhood, but when we meet him again, he is a young man, and it is revealed that God has given him an affinity for the Philistines because it is His plan to use him to destroy them.[121] However, Samson's desire to enjoy fleshly lusts causes him to repeatedly break the Nazarite vow that he was under from birth.[122] Yet we see that the favor of God is still upon him as he destroys the Philistines repeatedly in battle.[123] Only when he gave his heart to another instead of God did the favor lift off his life and his great strength was lost.[124] Now he and his God is made a mockery of by the Philistines.[125] This causes a man who has spent most of his life operating in partial and often complete disobedience to now willingly pray for help.[126] His embracing his purpose with a repentant heart causes God to answer his prayer, and in his death, he destroys more Philistines than he did during his entire lifetime.[127]

Samuel also came from a barren situation.[128] Unlike Samson, Samuel was raised in the house of God. Hannah, Samuel's mother, prayed earnestly concerning her barrenness and made a vow to the

Lord informing Him that if He allowed her to conceive and birth a son that she would give that son back to Him. Therefore, from the time Samuel was weened, he was given to the service of the Lord.[129] His relationship with God developed to the point that whenever he spoke, or prayed, God would eavesdrop to ensure that everything that came out of Samuel's mouth would be answered.[130] We learn from *NEW TESTAMENT SCRIPTURE* that when we pray according to the will of God that He hears us and gives us the answer to our prayer.[131] Samuel's entire life was wrapped around this *SCRIPTURE*. So much so that when he walked into a city people became fearful because they did not know if he was there to bless or curse the city.[132] All realized that if Samuel spoke it to the Father, it would come to pass. God used him to prove to us all that when we pray from a heart full of the will of God to be manifested in the earth, He will answer every prayer that we pray. His ears are attentive to those who truly love Him.[133]

God used the life of David to show us the importance of not becoming offended. Once one becomes offended, the spirit of retaliation envelops them, and they will not find peace until they have attacked the person who they believe wronged them. *SCRIPTURE* teaches that all offenses come from the spirit of the evil one because when one is offended, they tend to sin against the one who mistreated or offended them.[134] Therefore, the job of the enemy is to cause us to walk in offense. He knows that whenever we choose to retaliate, we are not allowing the Lord to fight our battles.[135] Whenever we retaliate, we lose. Whenever we stand still and see the salvation (deliverance) of the Lord, we win.[136] The only way we can successfully and continually do this is to remember that we are not wrestling against flesh and blood but against wicked spirits.[137] Although King Saul tried to kill David on many occasions, he refused to retaliate.[138] Even when given the opportunity to kill Saul on two different occasions, he refused.[139] He would not attack what God had once anointed. As a result, his prayers were answered, and God removed Saul and gave the blessing of Saul to David by making him king over all Israel.[140] We must remember that the wealth of the sinner is stored up for the just.[141] We get that wealth by choosing to not walk in offense. Furthermore, David never allowed the many attacks of King Saul to cause him to become offended and blame God either. His steadfastness to God and his trust in God's will and purpose being manifested in his life is an example that should be modeled by every believer. David's life is proof that all things work together for the good to those who love God and are called according to His purpose.

Solomon becomes an example of what occurs when we decide to pray for wisdom. Because his only desire was to operate under the Spirit of Wisdom, God promised him all the natural things that all others desire.[142] When we seek first the kingdom of God and its righteousness, God promised to add all the things of this world to us.[143] Although Solomon prayed this prayer, he allowed his desires of the flesh to deceive him and cause him to walk away from the Spirit of Wisdom and the plan of God for his life.[144] He allowed his lust of the flesh to overcome him, and he started marrying many women. His appetite for women only increased, and he begin to reach outside of Israel for women to marry, which was a violation of the covenant the nation of Israel had made with God. God told them that if they connected with those who were ungodly, it would affect them and cause them to become ungodly too.[145] The *NEW TESTAMENT* commands us to remain separated from those who walk in wickedness.[146] We are not to allow ourselves to become yoked up with them because, like Solomon, it will lead to our destruction.

One of the shortest of all prayers in the *BIBLE* occurs when Jabez asked God to enlarge his coasts.[147] His prayer was in alignment with the will and plan of God for all of Israel, so God answered. His example reveals that we determine what degree we operate within the kingdom of God. We should all want to maximize our time on earth by allowing the Lord to obtain our full consent to His purpose for our lives. We must all willingly pray that the Lord would enlarge our territory because the harvest is plentiful (great) but the laborers are few.[148] We should obey Jesus's command by praying to the Lord of the harvest to send laborers into His vineyard. However, it would be a travesty if we are not praying to be the laborer that He would continually send into His vineyards. Enlarge our ability to successfully reach and bring the lost into Your kingdom is our prayer.

God uses the life of the Prophet Isaiah to reveal one of the most important truths in all of *Scripture*. Isaiah was being used by God and was a prophet to the nation of Israel. However, he did not realize how corrupt he was until King Uzziah died. In his moment of grief, he saw the King of all kings, and in so doing, he was able to see himself.[149] He did not realize how corrupt he was. He stated that he was a man of unclean lips and that he lived amid people with unclean lips.[150] This is scary because he is speaking for God. After his conversion, he is showed multiple pictures of the Messiah. It is Isaiah that sees that a virgin shall conceive and give birth to a son.[151] From a natural perspective, we all know that this is impossible. However, what is impossible with humans is always possible with God.[152] Moreover, Isaiah is shown that the Messiah would hold the title and position as God the Father.[153] Furthermore, Isaiah is showed the kingdom of the Messiah and how He would save and deliver humanity by suffering the death of crucifixion.[154]

We meet Jeremiah as a young child. God calls him as a prophet to the nations by informing him that He knew him before He was even conceived.[155] *From God's perspective we learn that human life occurs prior to conception.* As a young child, Jeremiah made legitimate excuses as to why he was not capable of fulfilling his purpose or destiny. God responds by telling him not to look at the expressions on their faces but instead to do what He is telling him to do.[156] He further informs that his ministry will be one of throwing down and uprooting evil.[157] One would think that this information would cause him to understand that he is not going to be popular with people and that he would have to suffer persecution; however, Jeremiah did not seem to understand this. He is known as the *weeping prophet* because he spends so much time crying and complaining over the people not receiving the messages given to him by God, yet he is assured by God that he will be protected.[158] He is incarcerated and decides that he is going to give up and no longer be a prophet for God. His conversation/prayer with God is extremely interesting because of the seriousness of his heart. He says he is done. Then something occurs that he did not see coming. The *Bible* reveals that when he tried to stop speaking for God, there was a fire shut up inside his bones that compelled him to continue working for God.[159] His life is proof that even when we do not want to obey God by fulfilling His purpose for our lives, the right circumstances will usher us into His presence and thus cause us to change our minds and walk in complete obedience and surrender to God. The Prophet Jonah is another example of this truth. He decided to disobey God completely, and through circumstances beyond his control, he found himself in the belly of a great fish. While there, he began to repent, pray, and prophesy that he would see God's holy temple again.[160] He too repented and fulfilled his purpose by bringing revival to an entire nation.[161]

King Jehoshaphat is faced with three enemy nations preparing to attack Judah, and his actions reveal to us how we as believers are to deal with the attack of the enemy. He immediately calls the nation to prayer and fasting.[162] He then reminds God that when the Israelites came out of the wilderness, He would not allow them to destroy these three enemies.[163] He was not blaming God for the situation but rather informing Him that these enemies would have been dealt with hundreds of years earlier had He allowed. He was now praying for instruction on how to deal with this new threat. God's answer agreed with Jehoshaphat. God told him that they would not be required to fight these three enemy nations but that He would fight it for them.[164] The Lord caused the three enemies to destroy one another, and the Israelites were commanded to go in after the massacre to obtain the spoils of war.[165] It took them three days to remove the riches from the dead soldiers.[166] They then brought the spoils of war to the valley of Berachah, which means blessing, and worshipped Him.[167] The battle was won when they began to worship God, and the battle was concluded with them worshipping and blessing God in the *Valley of Blessing*. Worship, a form of prayer and adoration to the Lord, ensures victory. The true essence of prayer is understanding that God will always destroy every enemy that attacks us. Therefore, even in our imperfections and disobedience God always have a way of ensuring that His will for our lives will be accomplished.

CHAPTER 6

Intimacy with God (Part 1)

PRAYER IS THE ONLY WAY FOR THE believer to obtain intimacy with God. There are many forms of prayer as we have discovered throughout this book. Most importantly is our sincere desire to spend quality time with Him so that He can transform our nature and character. We must understand that spending time with Him occasionally is not enough if we want to be a light and example of His goodness in the earth. Additionally, we will not be able to fulfill the Great Commission of taking the *GOSPEL* of the kingdom into all the earth if we are not willing to spend intimate time with Him.[168] We must be willing to do whatever is required to hear the heart of God when it comes to reaching souls for Him. All believers should possess a hunger and thirst for righteousness to be established in every part of their lives.[169] This will lead them to spending more time with the Lord through prayer and the reading and studying of *HIS WORD*. Since prayer is not about asking God for stuff, but rather spending time in His presence, we as believers should make prayer a priority, knowing that the more time we spend in His presence, the more the anointing of the Anointed One (Jesus Christ) will rest upon our lives.

Unfortunately, many do not realize that prayer is God's way of ensuring that we will have an intimate relationship with Him. Most squander their time begging God for things that are not in *His Word* nor part of His will for them to have. Instead of developing this intimate life-changing relationship through the perseverance of submitting their will and plans to Him, they try to use Him as a Santa Claus or a genie. They want Him to give them their wants and their needs when they want them and most importantly how they want them. However, the *Scriptures* clearly teach that His sheep would know or be extremely and intimately acquainted with His voice so much so that they would never be deceived to follow the voice of a stranger.[170] This cannot occur if we are not spending large amounts of intimate time with our Lord.

The *Bible* states that after Enoch had a son named Methuselah, he began to walk with God.[171] Literally, it is revealed that he developed intimacy with God. He was just sixty-five years old when Methuselah was born, which was noticeably young to have children during this period of history. The *Word of God* does not detail what caused the change in his life. It does tell us that he had additional sons and daughters for the next three hundred years. During that three-hundred year span, he continued to develop his relationship with God to the point that he went to heaven without dying. According to *Hebrews 11:5*, Enoch's walk with God was based on faith. The more he spent time with God, the more he trusted Him. It is impossible for our personal faith to grow outside of spending time in the presence of God.

During those years of intimacy, obviously Enoch's character was being constantly changed. Spending that much time in the presence of a holy God could mean that he would wound up looking like, thinking like, talking like, and being like the One he was spending so much time with. Once he became one in character with the Father, he was translated from time into eternity, where he has been ever since. His desire to spend so much time with God caused him to get to heaven without dying. I am sure that was not his purpose for spending so much time with the Father. Instead, it reveals a longing and a lacking deep inside his being that caused him to understand that his purpose was tied to getting to know his Creator in a more intimate way. Enoch was not satisfied with mediocre existence. He was not satisfied with his relationship with God being like everyone else's. He was not trying to be like others nor was he willing to become a people pleaser. Enoch went against the norms of society. He stood out like a swollen finger on a hand. He was the only one in his generation willing to develop intimacy with the Father. His great-grandson Noah would be the next man who would desire intimacy with God.[172]

Therefore, if we as believers are going to please God, we must understand that as we seek intimacy with Him, we may find ourselves all alone in this quest. What I am saying is that, you may not know another person who is on this same quest as you. They may say with their mouth they are, but the fruit of their lives may reveal a different picture to you. However, it is not your place to become judgmental of others. Instead, it is your place to remain focused on your task, which is developing a daily and intimate relationship with the Creator of the universe; and you must be willing to constantly pray for them that the passion for God that lives in your heart is developed in theirs. Prayer is the foundation required to develop this relationship where we realize that it is a two-way conversation between the Creator and the created. We must spend time in His presence just listening for instruction and direction. We must willingly set time apart just for Him. The *SCRIPTURES* promise us that He knows our needs, and that He will meet or supply them.[173] Therefore, our primary goal in prayer should not be to tell Him what is on our mind but to hear what is on His mind. We should continually seek Him to find out what will bring Him joy. We should want to fulfill His plan for our lives to the point that nothing else matters. Jesus summed it up this way by saying, *"Not My will but Thine be done."*[174] We must be like Jesus and not just say these words, but really mean them. Only then will we experience the intimacy that God desires for us to have.

The first man, Adam, experience intimacy with God when God would walk with him in the cool of the day.[175] However, when we read about Adam and his encounter with God, we should immediately notice the absence of prayer. I am sure they conversated when they were together, but nowhere in the first three chapters of *GENESIS* do we see Adam praying to God when He is not there physically with him. Hindsight immediately reveal to us that this was a recipe for disaster. After Adam ate from the tree of the knowledge of good and evil, the *BIBLE* reveals that God came walking through the garden looking for him.[176] We notice from this that God was initiating the relationship of intimacy with Adam. Adam did not pray his way into the presence of God. Therefore, since he had nothing invested into initiating the relationship of intimacy, he had no problem lying to or blaming God for his sin. He hid himself from God because he was naked, and then he told God it was His fault by stating that the woman given to him by God gave him the fruit and he ate it.[177] Therefore, the woman followed suit and said it was the serpent's fault for beguiling (tricking) her.[178] The serpent is now quiet because anything not created in the image and likeness of God does not have permission to speak to Him without His permission. This is revealed in Job when God asks Satan a question on two different occasions.[179] Satan was not allowed to speak until given permission by God. That shows us how powerful the God we serve is and how powerless the enemy of our souls is. We have nothing to fear from the enemy. Our focus must remain on developing a more intimate relationship with our Lord and Savior, Jesus Christ. *SCRIPTURE* commands us to look away from (ignore) all that will distract and to focus our attention on Jesus, the Author and Finisher (Perfecter) of our faith.[180] Choosing to do this creates an atmosphere for the presence of God to be entered by each believer.[181] Step into His presence and allow Him to deliver you from all that life and the enemy have attempted to destroy your life and purpose. In His presence, those wounds will be healed, and you will walk in newness of life.[182]

Once we decide to chase God and His presence, we will find out that God is chasing after us too. The *BIBLE* reveals that we will reap what we have sown.[183] Therefore, going after God and His presence is a surefire guarantee that He will come after us. As we fight in prayer to enter His presence to develop intimacy with Him, we can be assured that He is fighting to enter our presence. We must remember that the Father entered the presence of Adam daily and walked with him in the cool of the day. There is a *"cool of the day"* moment in your life that God will access if you are willing to continue to seek Him with your whole heart. I must warn you that there are rules that must be adhered to ensure the continuation of this imitate relationship. Adam failed to consider this and lost the intimacy. In everyone's garden of peace (Eden) there will always be placed something that is forbidden for them to eat from.[184] This something was not created for you to feed from. Your nourishment is to come from other sources that your Creator has provided for you. In the *New Testament*, it is revealed that both the Father's and the Son's desire is to come into the presence of the believer so that They may dine with us.[185] Are you open to this level of intimacy?

Jesus developed intimacy with the Father when He was here on earth. Often, we miss the fact that He prayed to the Father. He gave us the example to follow, and most believers either do not understand what He was doing or why He was doing it. He would rise early in the morning and spend hours praying to the Father.[186] He maintained the intimate relationship that He and the Father had when He was with Him in heaven. Although He was living in a physical body, He understood the importance of prayer and intimacy with the Father. Although Jesus was fully God when He lived here on earth, He did nothing as God. Therefore, it was imperative to Him to spend as much time as possible in the presence of the Father, to ensure that He would only do the will of the Father. When He was in the garden of Gethsemane, He prayed to the Father for at least three hours. In severe agony, He prayed the same prayer multiple times.[187] The level of intimacy demonstrated there is amazing because of His willingness to submit His will to that of the Father although He realized the pain, agony, and separation from the Triune Godhead that was going to occur.[188] He spent this much time in prayer while His disciples were asleep. He pushed pass His feelings of tiredness and despair so that He could have an audience with the Father. Following His example will cause us to push past our emotions and physical relationships to get into a place where we are willing to surrender our dreams, plans, and desires to the Father.

We have consistently talked about entering (resting in) the presence of God at a general level, but now we will move into how to accomplish this in a very practical way from a *scriptural* perspective.

We understand from the *BIBLE* that all can come to God with a repentant heart.[189] When this is done, salvation is received. According to the *WORD OF GOD*, this is the primary prayer that God hears from the sinner.[190] Unfortunately, most do not realize this, and many are angry with God for not answering their prayers when they have not done self-inventory of their lives. Many have a head knowledge of salvation but have not allowed that knowledge to produce change in the heart of their spirits. There is no real difference between how they live their day-to-day lives from that of those who claim no relationship with the Lord Jesus Christ. They may read their *BIBLES* and go to church on Sunday, but their lifestyle never changes. They believe they are saved (born again), but from what the *BIBLE* teaches, they only have a form of godliness, and their very lifestyles deny the power associated with the conversion we call salvation.[191] They find themselves in and out with God. They pray without success and find themselves frustrated. They do not realize or understand that God only hears the prayers of those who are part of His kingdom, and since they are on the outside looking in, He is not required to answer them, although He rains on the just as well as the unjust.[192] Because of His unconditional love, they will get a little rain sprinkled upon their lives but never the downpouring of blessing and favor that He desires to give them. Those who are born again must willingly share the good news of the kingdom with those who are stuck in this cycle of frustration so that they can experience the salvation that Christ has made available to them.

The *BIBLE* teaches that those entering the presence of God must be covered. We first see this when God is establishing the rules of engagement when it comes to entering His presence. He told Moses in the book of *EXODUS* who would be able to enter and what was required. He went into detail explaining what the priests would have to do physically and what they would be required to wear when operating in His presence.[193] Most call the edifice that was constructed the tabernacle of Moses, but the truth is that, it is the tabernacle of God because God instructed Moses to build it based upon a pattern that exists in heaven.[194] The priest had to wear certain clothing or covering when going into the tabernacle. Once we realize that going into the tabernacle is another way of saying going into the presence of God spiritually speaking, we will begin to understand that we cannot enter His presence uncovered or dressed improperly.

CHAPTER 7

Intimacy with God (Part 2)

*S*CRIPTURE REVEAL THAT THERE ARE FOUR COVERINGS required to enter the presence of God. First, *ROMANS 13:14* commands all to "*put on*" the Lord Jesus Christ. As stated previously, salvation is a requirement to enter the presence of God. Head knowledge is not enough. Accepting the gift of salvation given by our Lord by His death on the cross produces permanent change in the heart of our spirits. We become new creations in Christ Jesus. Our new desire is to be like Him. We willingly allow our character and nature to be reprogrammed into what is pleasing to Him. No longer do we have an opinion on how we should live or what we should do, but we look to the *WORD OF GOD* for direction in every area of our lives.[195] Whenever we find a part of our lives not in alignment with *HIS WORD* we change. Our great love for Him is continually developed as we grow in the knowledge and grace of the Lord Jesus Christ. Being a new creation in Christ Jesus causes us to separate ourselves from the influence of those who have chosen to remain a part of the kingdom of darkness.[196] We move from the broad path that leads to eternal death and destruction and move to the straight and narrow path that leads to eternal life.[197] Our primary focus is only growing and learning His ways. Therefore, we desire the sincere milk of *HIS WORD* so that we may grow and develop in a way that is pleasing to Him.[198] We crucify the deeds of our flesh by walking in the Spirit daily.[199] We allow the *BIBLE* to become our final authority instead of our opinion or, more tragically, the opinions of others. True salvation is evidenced or on display based on our willingness to obey *HIS WORD*. Jesus stated in *JOHN 14:15* and *JOHN 14:23–24* that those who genuinely love Him will keep His commandments. Once salvation is experienced in the heart of the believer, the only desire followed is to please the Father.

Secondly, *ISAIAH 61:3* commands the believer to *"put on"* the garment of praise for the spirit of heaviness. One would think that accepting Jesus Christ as Lord and Savior would remove all heaviness (depression). However, we see from this *SCRIPTURE* that the praise of the believer is used to attack the spirit of depression. In our society, depression is an epidemic. People are medicated at many different levels to deal with the feelings of depression that they are experiencing. Depression is real, but praise God, it is treatable, especially for the believer. As followers of Jesus Christ, we do not have to medicate ourselves with physical drugs obtained from a medical doctor, but we can access the Doctor of all doctors and allow Him to heal us. Please notice from the above *SCRIPTURE* that we have been given a weapon to combat depression. Praise is not just something we do, but it is a weapon to attack the very thing that is attacking our souls. Although most understand what it means to praise something or someone, we will take a moment to develop a working definition of the word so that we are all on the same page. *Praise means that we will esteem greatness to our God, we will be thankful to Him for being who He is, and we will worship Him for His unconditional love demonstrated toward us although we realize we only deserve His judgment.* Please notice that this definition of praise has nothing to with whether you got your prayers answered. Most Christians have been programmed to only praise God if they get the new job, new car, new spouse, or healing. However, praise is something that occurs based on your love and reverence of Him and not what you are able to obtain from Him. This explains why many have struggled to develop intimacy with God. They love God and work diligently to enter His presence only to find that in the back of their mind they are upset with Him for not answering their prayer about whatever they believe they should have obtained from Him. This hinders their ability to receive His unconditional love, and they walk away frustrated instead of fulfilled.

Praise is the antidote for depression. This explains why Satan always try to get us to complain about what we are going through. He makes sure that when we are in the struggle that we never consider *ROMANS 8:28*. We have a promise from the God who created and sustains the entire universe that He is working all things together for our good because we love Him and are the called according to His purpose. Our love is demonstrated by our obedience. When walking in obedience you will willingly answer when He calls your name. He has chosen you for greatness, but it will never be experienced if you do not answer the call. The garment of praise when used properly will usher you into the presence of God. *ISAIAH 61:6* states that those who wear the garment of praise are priests of the Lord. This means that those of us who willingly praise God instead of living in depression have access to the presence of God. *Intimacy with God is the cure for all that ails us.* The will of God for all believers is to be grateful and thankful.[200] Wearing this garment dispels all that the enemy is trying to do in our lives. The Israelites spent forty years in the wilderness because of their refusal to be grateful and thankful to God. Although they had witnessed God bring ten plagues upon the Egyptians, His parting of the Red Sea and drowning their enemies, they still complained. After complaining ten different times, God passed judgment upon them and informed them that the blessing He had for them would not be experienced by them but by their children. He told them they would walk in circles until they died.[201] They loved depression more than praise, and they lived the rest of their lives trapped in it while watching their children leave that spirit behind and step into a realm of praising God.

Thirdly, according to *COLOSSIANS 3:10–17* we have been commanded to "*put on*" the garment of the fruit of the Spirit. Throughout this book, we have been teaching the concept that spending time in the presence of God will cause the nature and character of Christ to be developed in the heart of the believer. The above *SCRIPTURE* commands us to make sure that the character of Christ is being developed in our hearts. A good idea becomes a God idea when it is expressly revealed in *His Word*. We must willingly *"put on"* as a garment or covering the fruit of the Spirit. The first two garments we were commanded to put on dealt with our relationship with God. The next two garments we are commanded to put on deal with our relationship with people. The purpose for the fruit of the Spirit is to teach us how to treat others. God's plan is for us to wear His character so that all who we meet experience Him and not us. We all know that we are often on an emotional rollercoaster, and if we are caught at the wrong time, we will say something or do something that will cause unnecessary pain to those we encounter. No one deserves to ride on the rollercoaster of confusion and frustration that we often demonstrate. Although we are working diligently to walk in the Spirit, unfortunately sometimes our emotions come through. At these times, we must make sure that only the fruit of the Spirit is flowing through us so that we do not accidently harm people by becoming a stumbling block to their developing their own personal relationship with the Lord Jesus Christ.[202]

Putting on the character of the Lord Jesus Christ means that we will love people unconditionally because we realize that this is how He loves us. We will develop patience in dealing with people. We will instantly forgive those who have mistreated us. We will operate in meekness when every fiber of our being may be telling us to retaliate. Meekness means we have strength, but we never lose control. We will allow the Lord to bring vengeance on those who have mistreated us, and we will pray for them as He has commanded.[203] We will be kind to all people whether we feel they deserve it or not. We will live a life of humility because we understand that if God treated us as we deserved, we would be burning in hell right now. Our appreciation for His unconditional love and forgiveness causes us to be so grateful and thankful that we willingly share His love with all that we encounter.

Fourth, we have been challenged through *Scripture* to *"put on"* the whole or complete armor of God so that we will no longer be deceived by the tricks and schemes of the wicked one. Although wearing the armor of God provides an additional level of protection for the believer, the main purpose is not to protect you as you rest in His presence, but to protect you as you go forth in spiritual warfare to free those who are being oppressed by the devil. *EPHESIANS 6:10–18* document instructions to believers who have developed such an intimate walk with God that they want what God wants, which is souls brought into His kingdom. Those who have placed the will of the Father above their own will gladly wear the armor of God and risk encounters with the kingdom of darkness so that all humans can experience the same level of freedom in Jesus that they daily enjoy. *SCRIPTURE* informs that the Son offers freedom to all who are oppressed by the devil.[204] He wants all believers to work with Him so that the captives can be freed.[205] It is very subtle, and therefore, it can be easily overlooked. The armor belongs to God, and because He loves humanity so much, He allows us to wear it to pull or snatch them out of whatever sin or stronghold Satan has trapped them in. We should consider it an honor and privilege that our intimacy with our Heavenly Father has positioned us in a place where He trusts us enough to provide us with such a life-changing gift that can be used to help hurt and mistreated people.

Therefore, putting on the armor of God gives the believer the ability to stand firm against whatever the enemy is throwing at them. First, we must wear the belt of truth when snatching souls out of the fire.[206] When reading the *BIBLE*, it becomes apparent that human's greatest weakness seems to deal with their sexuality. Many of the greatest men of the *BIBLE* succumbed to this struggle.[207] Therefore, as believers we must make it a point of emphasis to allow God to deliver us in this area. Otherwise, when we go out to help others, we could become tempted by their appearance, whether physical, mental, or emotional, and fall into the temptation. Wearing the breastplate of righteousness ensures that you will retain your integrity when temptation comes. Righteousness means that you have been justified or placed in right standing with God and you are not willing to do anything that will remove you from that place of favor.[208] Next, we must willingly have our feet covered with the *GOSPEL* of peace so that we can share a balanced *GOSPEL* with those who are lost. We must tell them that, although they deserve the wrath of God because of their sins, He is coming to them with a treaty of peace.[209] He wants to end the war that they have been in against Him.

The shield of faith quenches all the fiery darks of Satan. Please understand that spending time with God increases our trust (faith) in Him. This element of covering is so important that the SCRIPTURE states above all else have your shield of faith active when you are snatching souls out of the fires of hell.[210] Next, we must wear the helmet of salvation. The spirit of every believer is renewed through the miracle of salvation. However, our minds must be transformed by the WORD OF GOD.[211] Thus, we must prayerfully spend time with God in HIS WORD if we desire transformation to occur. Spending time with God will teach us how to use HIS WORD in warfare. HIS WORD is a sword, which informs that it destroys what it cuts. We do not want to make the mistake that Peter made in the garden of Gethsemane and cut who we believe is the enemy when we have been informed that our battle is not against flesh and blood.[212] Therefore, we must remain alert by allowing the spirit of discernment to operate in our lives so that we will know how to properly pray for those who are oppressed by the devil. We must allow the Lord to teach us how to be skillful as we through warfare prayer pull souls out of the kingdom of darkness and into the kingdom of His Son.[213]

Having an intimate walk with God is attainable for all Christians. Unfortunately, most never consider doing the work required to obtain this level of relationship with the Father and Son. Yet we have been instructed to work out our own salvation with fear and trembling.[214] Intimacy requires discipline and dedication. The Holy Spirit has been given to the believer to usher us into the presence of the Father and the Son. Although the Holy Spirit is God, the BIBLE reveals that He would not speak of Himself but would only speak what the Father and the Son are revealing.[215] The Holy Spirit is God on earth who comes to live within the heart (spirit) of the believer to lead, guide, and direct us into all truth.[216] It is impossible to develop a vibrant relationship with the Lord without learning the art of communication. This art is only developed through spending lengthy times of prayer with the Father. As stated throughout this book, prayer cannot be just about making requests to the Lord. It must be deeper than that. It must be based on a personal relationship built from a place of genuine appreciation and love for the One who created you. The unconditional love being experienced from both sides develops a level of intimacy which words cannot truly explain.

Walking intimately with God implies that you love being in His presence. SCRIPTURE states that two cannot walk together except there be agreement between them.[217] Since God is holy, we know He will never lower His standards to fit our warped opinion of how things should be. Therefore, we as believers must be willing to conform our will to His for there to be a true meeting of the minds. The meeting of the minds is the real challenge that must be considered if oneness is ever going to occur with God. If we cannot achieve oneness of mind and purpose with God, we can be assured that we will never be able to accomplish it with others. The reason this is important is because some things are not handled in the spirit realm until there is agreement between humans who choose to pray to the Father in the name of Jesus.[218] When our vertical relationship with God is right, it assures us that we can have horizontal relationships with other Christians that will please the Lord. We must remember that the WORD OF GOD declares that one will put one thousand demons to flight but two will put ten thousand demons to flight.[219] The power of agreement in prayer is our secret weapon to break generational curses and pull down strongholds that the enemy have established in the lives of hurting people.

Developing intimacy in prayer ensures proper relationship with the Father. Also, it gives God a weapon that He can use to bring others out of darkness and into His kingdom. You become an instrument of righteousness that the Father can use to snatch souls out of the fire.[220] Selfless prayer is the language of God. As you spend most of your time praying for others, you can be assured that God will engage the LAW of reciprocity in your life, and He will cause you to reap all the prayer blessings that you have prayed to manifest in the lives of others. Therefore, enter His presence through the doorway of prayer. He and a lost world are waiting for you!

Introduction

[1] *PSALM 138:2*
[2] *ISAIAH 55:1–7; JOHN 15:1–6; JAMES 4:6–8; REVELATION 3:20–21*
[3] *MATTHEW 7:13–14*
[4] *GALATIANS 6:1–2*
[5] *LUKE 11:1*

Chapter 1: Purpose of Prayer

[6] *PSALM 37:4*
[7] *MATTHEW 7:7–8; LUKE 11:9–10*
[8] *1 JOHN 1:9*
[9] *JOHN 3:16–21; JOHN 3:35–36*
[10] *MATTHEW 5:43–44*
[11] *ROMANS 12:14*
[12] *DEUTERONOMY 6:5; MATTHEW 22:37; MARK 12:30; LUKE 10:27; ROMANS 5:8*
[13] *MATTHEW 26:39, 26:42; LUKE 22:42*
[14] *ISAIAH 40:31; PSALM 100:2*
[15] *MATTHEW 9:36–38*
[16] *ROMANS 12:1–2; PHILIPPIANS 2:5; 1 PETER 1:13*
[17] *COLOSSIANS 1:9–13*
[18] *JOHN 5:17–20, 8:28–30, 8:37–40*
[19] *PSALM 95:6–11; JOHN 10:1–6, 10:14–18, 10:24–30*
[20] *JOSHUA 24:14–27; 1 SAMUEL 12:14–15; 2 CHRONICLES 7:12–14*
[21] *PHILIPPIANS 4:19; 1 JOHN 5:14–15*
[22] *ISAIAH 1:18–20*

Chapter 2: Hindrances to Prayer

23 *2 Corinthians 5:17*
24 *Jude 1:20–21*
25 *Matthew 7:12; Luke 6:31*
26 *Proverbs 18:20–21; Matthew 12:37*
27 *Genesis 2:9, 3:22–24; Revelation 2:7, 22:2, 22:14*
28 *Proverbs 11:30*
29 *Genesis 1:26–28*
30 *Genesis 2:15–17*
31 *John 6:63*
32 *John 5:17–20, 8:28–30, 8:37–40*
33 *Proverbs 18:4; Ephesians 5:26*
34 *Philippians 4:13*
35 *James 1:5–8*
36 *Psalm 103:20*
37 *2 Corinthians 5:7*
38 *James 3:8; Acts 2:4, 10:46, 19:6*
39 *Matthew 12:34; Luke 6:45*
40 *1 Peter 3:10*

Chapter 3: Blueprint for Prayer

41 *Exodus 25:9, 25:40; Hebrews 8:5*
42 *Exodus 25:1–40, 26:1–37, 27:1–21, 28:1–43*
43 *Colossians 1:12–20*
44 *Luke 11:1*
45 *Matthew 14:23; Mark 1:35, 6:46, 14:32–39; Luke 5:16, 6:12, 9:18*
46 *Matthew 6:9; Luke 11:2*
47 *Jeremiah 29:11–13*
48 *3 John 1:2*
49 *Matthew 6:14–15*

Chapter 4: Types of Prayer

50 *1 Thessalonians 5:17*
51 *Luke 18:1*
52 *Matthew 6:8; Philippians 4:19*
53 *Genesis 22:11–14*
54 *Matthew 3:1–2, 4:17*

55 *ROMANS 3:23*
56 *1 JOHN 1:8*
57 *JOHN 8:4–11*
58 *1 CORINTHIANS 10:13*
59 *JAMES 5:16*
60 *PROVERBS 27:17*
61 *GALATIANS 6:7*
62 *EPHESIANS 1:3, 2:6*
63 *MATTHEW 6:10*
64 *PSALM 115:16*
65 *MATTHEW 16:19*
66 *JAMES 5:15*
67 *MATTHEW 26:11; MARK 14:7; JOHN 12:8*
68 *GALATIANS 3:13*
69 *PHILIPPIANS 4:6*
70 *PHILIPPIANS 4:19*
71 *MALACHI 3:10–11*
72 *MATTHEW 15:22–28; MARK 7:24–30*
73 *PSALM 23:5; 2 SAMUEL 9:1–13*
74 *PROVERBS 16:2, 21:2*
75 *1 THESSALONIANS 5:18*
76 *MATTHEW 26:36–44; LUKE 22:39–46; JOHN 18:1–11*
77 *JEREMIAH 29:11–13*
78 *MATTHEW 5:43–44; LUKE 6:27–28; ROMANS 12:14*
79 *EPHESIANS 6:12*
80 *PSALM 7:1–17, 55:1–23, 69:1–36*
81 *1 PETER 5:7*
82 *ISAIAH 40:31*
83 *GENESIS 11:1–9*
84 *1 CORINTHIANS 12:14–27*
85 *DEUTERONOMY 32:30; JOSHUA 23:9–11*
86 *MATTHEW 18:20*
87 *JAMES 4:12*
88 *1 TIMOTHY 2:1–2*
89 *JOHN 14:16–18, 15:26–27, 16:7, 16:13*
90 *JOHN 14:17*
91 *JOHN 14:26–27*
92 *1 CORINTHIANS 14:1–29, 14:39–40*
93 *ROMANS 8:26–27*
94 *MATTHEW 6:10*
95 *REVELATION 4:1–11, 5:1–14*
96 *1 CORINTHIANS 14:15*

Chapter 5: Prayers in the Bible

97 *1 John 5:14–15*
98 *Genesis 12:4–5*
99 *Genesis 12:1*
100 *Genesis 12:4*
101 *Genesis 13:7–12*
102 *Genesis 15:1–3*
103 *Genesis 15:4–21*
104 *Genesis 16:1–4*
105 *Genesis 16:11–16*
106 *Genesis 17:15–22*
107 *Genesis 17:9–14*
108 *Exodus 2:2*
109 *Exodus 2:5–10*
110 *Exodus 2:11–12*
111 *Exodus 2:21–22, 18:2–6*
112 *Exodus 3:4–10*
113 *Exodus 4:14–15*
114 *Exodus 32:19–20; Numbers 20:7–12*
115 *Numbers 11:10–15*
116 *Exodus 32:7–10*
117 *Exodus 32:11–14; Numbers 14:11–19, 21:6–9*
118 *Numbers 27:15–23*
119 *Judges 13:1–2*
120 *Judges 13:3–5; Numbers 6:1–21*
121 *Judges 14:1–4*
122 *Judges 14:5–9, 15:14–17, 16:1*
123 *Judges 14:19, 15:7–8, 15:14–17*
124 *Judges 16:16–20*
125 *Judges 16:21–25*
126 *Judges 16:28*
127 *Judges 16:29–30*
128 *1 Samuel 1:1–2, 1:5–6*
129 *1 Samuel 1:9–28*
130 *1 Samuel 3:19*
131 *1 John 5:14–15*
132 *1 Samuel 16:4–5*
133 *Nehemiah 1:6, 1:11; Psalm 130:2*
134 *Matthew 16:23; Romans 5:16–18, 16:17*
135 *Exodus 15:3; 1 Samuel 17:47; 2 Chronicles 20:15*
136 *2 Chronicles 20:17*
137 *2 Corinthians 10:3–6*

138 *1 Samuel 18:11, 18:13, 19:10, 19:11, 19:18*
139 *1 Samuel 24:1–22, 26:1–25*
140 *2 Samuel 5:1–5*
141 *Proverbs 13:22*
142 *1 Kings 3:7–15; 2 Chronicles 1:7–12*
143 *Matthew 6:33*
144 *1 Kings 11:1–13; Nehemiah 13:26*
145 *Deuteronomy 7:1–6*
146 *2 Corinthians 6:14–18*
147 *1 Chronicles 4:9–10*
148 *Matthew 9:37–38; Luke 10:2*
149 *Isaiah 6:1–5*
150 *Isaiah 6:5–8*
151 *Isaiah 7:14–16*
152 *Genesis 18:14; Jeremiah 32:17; Matthew 19:26; Mark 9:23, 10:27; Luke 1:37*
153 *Isaiah 9:6–7*
154 *Isaiah 52:13–16, 53:1–12*
155 *Jeremiah 1:4–5*
156 *Jeremiah 1:6–9*
157 *Jeremiah 1:10*
158 *Jeremiah 15:19–21, 20:1–6, 38:1–6*
159 *Jeremiah 20:7–11*
160 *Jonah 2:1–7*
161 *Jonah 3:3–10*
162 *2 Chronicles 20:1–3*
163 *2 Chronicles 20:5–12*
164 *Exodus 15:3; 1 Samuel 17:47; 2 Chronicles 20:15*
165 *2 Chronicles 20:22–24*
166 *2 Chronicles 20:25*
167 *2 Chronicles 20:26*

Chapter 6: Intimacy with God (Part 1)

168 *Matthew 28:18–20; Mark 16:15–16*
169 *Matthew 5:6*
170 *John 10:3–5, 10:14*
171 *Genesis 5:21–22*
172 *Genesis 6:7–8*
173 *Philippians 4:19*
174 *Matthew 26:39, 26:42; Luke 22:42*
175 *Genesis 3:8*
176 *Genesis 3:9*

177 *Genesis 3:10–12*
178 *Genesis 3:13*
179 *Job 1:6–8, 2:1–3*
180 *Hebrews 12:2*
181 *Psalm 100:1–6*
182 *Romans 6:4; 2 Corinthians 5:17*
183 *2 Corinthians 9:6; Galatians 6:7–8*
184 *Genesis 2:15–17*
185 *Revelation 3:20*
186 *Matthew 14:23; Mark 1:35, 6:46, 14:32–39; Luke 5:16, 6:12, 9:18*
187 *Matthew 26:39, 26:42; Luke 22:42*
188 *Hebrews 12:2*
189 *Matthew 3:2, 4:17; Mark 1:15*
190 *Acts 2:37–41*
191 *2 Timothy 3:1–5*
192 *Matthew 5:45*
193 *Exodus 28:1–43*
194 *Exodus 26:30; Hebrews 8:5*

Chapter 7: Intimacy with God (Part 2)

195 *Proverbs 3:5–6*
196 *2 Corinthians 6:14–18*
197 *Matthew 7:13–14*
198 *1 Peter 2:1–3*
199 *Galatians 5:14–26*
200 *1 Thessalonians 5:18*
201 *Numbers 14:26–35*
202 *Leviticus 19:14; Romans 14:13; 1 Corinthians 8:9; 1 John 2:10*
203 *Matthew 5:43–44; Romans 12:14*
204 *John 8:36*
205 *Mark 16:17–20*
206 *Jude 1:22–23*
207 *Genesis 38:13–26; Judges 16:1; 2 Samuel 11:1–5; 1 Kings 11:1–13*
208 *Romans 3:20–26, 5:1–2, 5:8–9, 8:28–30; 1 Corinthians 6:9–11*
209 *Isaiah 9:6; Romans 15:33, 16:20; 2 Corinthians 13:11; Philippians 4:9; 2 Thessalonians 3:16; Hebrews 13:20–21*
210 *Jude 1:22–23*
211 *Romans 12:1–2*
212 *John 18:10–11; Matthew 26:51–53; Mark 14:47; Luke 22:49–51*
213 *Colossians 1:13*
214 *Philippians 2:12*

[215] *John 14:26, 16:13*
[216] *John 16:13*
[217] *Amos 3:3*
[218] *Matthew 18:18–20*
[219] *Deuteronomy 32:30*
[220] *Jude 1:22–23*

Apostle Darryl L. Gay is the founder and senior pastor of The Tabernacle of Tuscaloosa. He has faithfully served in this role since April 1999. Although he continues to work a full-time job as a senior information security analyst, he still finds time to assist his parishioners with their daily, weekly, or monthly issues. He is always a phone call away from addressing whatever issue they are facing by providing biblical solutions. The wisdom imparted in his heart by the Holy Spirit has assisted his local congregation and many others to make the correct life decisions to positively impact their future so they can fulfill their God-given purpose and destiny. His passion for Christ is contagious, and many have accepted and followed Jesus Christ because of the example he continues to set. His love for the Lord has caused him to even make himself available to the family members of his parishioners who are often located all over the country and world. He tirelessly works with any that society has given up on to offer them hope and to challenge them to dream again by helping them to understand that they were created with purpose and for a purpose, and his mission is to help them find and fulfill their purpose.

To learn more about the ministry of Pastor Darryl L. Gay please visit www.TheTabernacle.net.

9 798886 162615